P9-DMY-514

Children of the World

Burma

FRANKLIN PIERCE
COLLEGE LIBRARY
RINDGE, N.H. 03461

Note: As this book goes to press (June 1989), the Burmese government has announced that the official names of the country and places within it have been changed to more accurately reflect native pronunciation. As a result, Burma is now officially known as the Union of Myanmar (mee-ahn-MAH). The country's capital, Rangoon, is now known as Yangon (yahn-KOH). We will incorporate these changes in future printings of this book.

For their help in the preparation of *Children of the World: Burma*, the editors gratefully thank Ko Chen Aye, Marquette University; the Embassy of Burma (Canada), Ottawa; the Embassy of Burma (US), Washington, DC; and the International Institute of Wisconsin, Milwaukee.

British Library Cataloguing in Publication Data
Burma.
1. Burma. Social life
I. Morieda, Takashi II. Knowlton, MaryLee, 1946-
III. Sachner, Mark J., 1948-   IIII. Series
959.1'05

ISBN 0-83687-068-9

This UK edition first published in 1989 by
Gareth Stevens Children's Books
31 Newington Green, London N16 9PU

This work was originally published in shortened form consisting of section I only.
Photographs and original text copyright © 1986 Takashi Morieda.
First and originally published by Kaisei-sha Publishing Co., Ltd., Tokyo.
World English rights arranged with Kaisei-sha Publishing Co., Ltd. through
Japan Foreign-Rights Centre.

Copyright this format © 1987 by Gareth Stevens, Inc.
Additional material and maps copyright © 1987 by Gareth Stevens, Inc.

All rights reserved. No part of this book may be reproduced in any form or by any means without permission in writing from Gareth Stevens, Inc.

CURR
DS.9
527.9
B87
.1989

Editor (UK): John O'Brien
Map design: Gary Moseley

Printed in the United States of America

1 2 3 4 5 6 7 8 9 95 94 93 92 91 90 89

Children of the World

Burma

Photography
by Takashi Morieda

Edited by
MaryLee Knowlton &
Mark J. Sachner

Gareth Stevens Children's Books
LONDON • MILWAUKEE

. . . a note about *Children of the World*:

The children of the world live in fishing towns and urban centres, on islands and in mountain valleys, on sheep ranches and fruit farms. This series follows one child in each country through the pattern of his or her life. Candid photographs show the children with their families, at school, at play, and in their communities. The text describes the dreams of the children and, often through their own words, tells how they see themselves and their lives.

Each book also explores events that are unique to the country in which the child lives, including festivals, religious ceremonies, and national holidays. The *Children of the World* series does more than tell about foreign countries. It introduces the children of each country and shows readers what it is like to be a child in that country.

. . . and about *Burma*:

Thet Way and his family live near the city of Rangoon, the capital of Burma. A major focus of Thet Way's life is the Buddhist religion. A special ceremony initiating Thet Way into the religion is featured in this book. Thet Way is also like children all over the world. He likes to play a Burmese version of marbles or shoot a catapult made for him by his father, a carpenter.

To enhance this book's value in libraries and classrooms, comprehensive reference sections include up-to-date data about Burma's geography, demographics, language, currency, education, culture, industry, and natural resources. *Burma* also features a bibliography, research topics, activity projects, and discussions of such subjects as Rangoon, the country's history, political system, ethnic and religious composition, and language.

The living conditions and experiences of children in Burma vary tremendously according to economic, environmental, and ethnic situations. The reference sections help bring to life for younger readers the diversity and richness of the culture and heritage of Burma. Of particular interest are discussions of the variety of cultures that have made their presence felt in the language and tradition of Burma.

CONTENTS

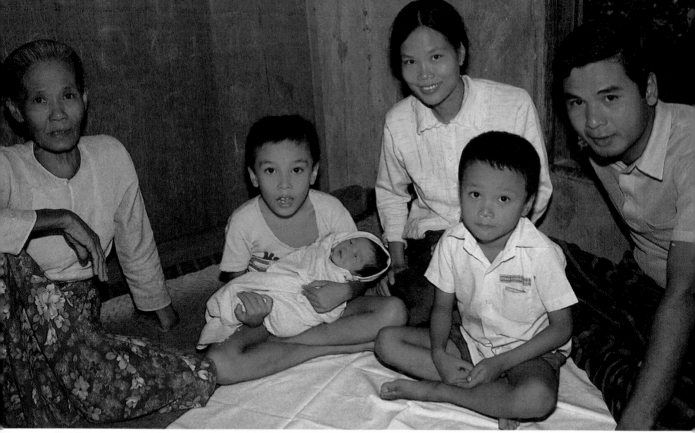

Holding his new baby sister, Thet Way sits with his grandmother, his mother and father, and his younger brother Thet Nay.

LIVING IN BURMA:
Thet Way, a Buddhist Boy

Thet Way is a nine-year-old boy. He lives in Hninzigen. Hninzigen is a suburb of Rangoon, the capital city of Burma.

Thet Way's family consists of his parents, himself, his six-year-old brother Thet Nay, and his baby sister Choe Nwe Soe. Thet Way's grandmother has come from the countryside to stay for a while. She is helping her daughter with the new baby. Thet Way is thrilled to have a baby sister. He and Thet Nay love to hold and hug her.

The village of Mouywa, north of Rangoon in Upper Burma. This is where Thet Way's parents — and Thet Way too — were born. Poor rainfall limits rice crops to one harvest a year in Upper Burma. That is why many farmers and other workers move south to Rangoon.

Thet Way's Parents at Work

Thet Way's father, U Tin, was once a farmer from Mouywa. Mouywa is a village in Upper Burma. When he started his family, he did not have enough land to raise food for his whole family. So he left his native village and came to the big city of Rangoon to make a living.

In Rangoon, U Tin learned that he needed a special skill. The city was filled with people like him. They, too, were from the countryside. And they also wanted to start a new life. So U Tin became a carpenter.

Thet Way helps out by carrying bamboo for his father's chairs.

U Tin makes chairs from bamboo. He makes the chairs — adult chairs, children's chairs, desk chairs, and dining chairs — in his home workshop.

His tools for making chairs are simple — a saw and a hammer. It is his skill that makes them special. First he shapes the frame. Then he puts in the seat and the back. On the back, he carves the designs that make his chairs unique. Because of the carving, he can make just two chairs a day.

When U Tin has made enough chairs, he takes them off to the market. He carries them across his shoulder. They dangle from a thick bamboo stick. The chairs are very popular in the market. They cost 30 to 40 *kyat* ('chat'). This comes to about £3. Other chairs are made of teak or other wood. They cost about £20. He sells 30 to 40 chairs a month.

Today Thet Way helps his father by carrying in bamboo boards. His father says that in his native village a boy Thet Way's age would do the work of a man. Thet Way only works when he wants pocket money!

Thet Way's father on his way to sell his chairs.

Thet Way's mother prepares tanaka.

Thet Way's mother sells *tanaka* in the market every morning. Tanaka is a branch. People grate it and mix it with water to make it into a lotion. The lotion is used to make a powder. People put the powder on their faces. It refreshes them in hot weather.

Thet Way's mother finds the tanaka. She cuts the branches into useful sizes. She then dries them, puts them into a basket, and carries them on her head to the market.

She sells her tanaka in the marketplace.

The boys sleep on a mat made of knitted bamboo skin spread over a wooden bed.

At Home in the Morning

The day starts early in Burma, as in most hot countries. Getting up early lets people finish their work when it is still cool. Thet Way gets up at six o'clock. By then, his mother is already making breakfast, and his father is getting supplies together.

Getting dressed in the morning is easy. The boys wear the clothes they slept in! People in Burma bathe several times a day. The water is kept in a drum in the backyard, and everyone washes right there. For now, Thet Way and his brother wash their faces in the water drum, and they're ready. Then they're off to the market to buy some fried food for breakfast.

Thet Way washes his face at the water drum.

Mixing spices and herbs. Thet Way enjoys preparing sauces, and he often helps his mother cook.

Thet Way's grandma pours off the water from the boiling rice.

Thet Way's mother cooks over a charcoal fire.

Thet Way samples some food.

Thet Way eats from a large bowl with his hand. Burmese say the hand can taste. So except for soup, they eat all their food with their hands. Thet Way has a bowl of rice for every meal. He also eats a mixture of shrimp, salt, garlic, onion, and chili peppers. They are pounded into a paste. The dish is served at almost every meal. It goes well with rice and fried fish. Like most Burmese, Thet Way loves hot food. He can even eat fresh hot pepper!

Tonight's menu: fried chicken, green mango salad, shrimp curry, bean soup, and grated shrimp.

Burmese love rice, and, like East Indians, they usually eat with their fingers.

Thet Nay feeds the chickens in the back of the house.

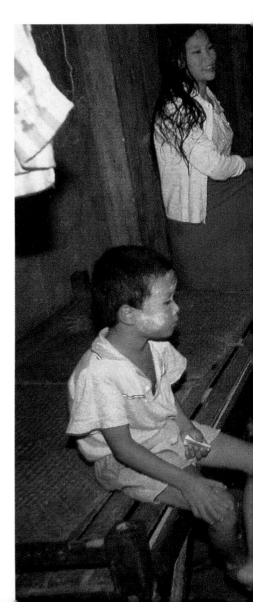

The traditional Burmese house is built of wood. Its lower floor is well off the ground. Thet Way's family lives on the ground floor of a two-storied house. The walls of the ground floor are made of concrete. The owner lives upstairs. Half the downstairs is used as a kitchen and sleeping place for his mother and baby sister.

16

The other half of the house is the living room. This is the centre of family life. It is a study for Thet Way and his brother, a workshop for their father, a family dining room, and a bedroom for the boys and their father. The door is always open. The neighbours drop by to chat or play or share a cup of tea. Thet Way's friends come by to take a nap there, even when he's not in. Everybody is friendly to one another. It's as if they all belong to one big family.

The living room: a place for working, relaxing, eating, and sleeping.

Two of the main features of Burma's landscape: a river and dense forest.

About half of Burma is covered with forests.

Going into Hninzigen

Hninzigen used to be just a village. Today it is a township made up of many villages. Some are residential and some are farm villages. Besides Burmese nationals, the town is home to Mon and Karen people. The people of Hninzigen support their families in many ways. Some keep water buffaloes to till their rice paddies. Others work in offices in Rangoon. Some sell goods at the market. Others, like Thet Way's father, make things at home.

Near Thet Way's house is a government office. It rations supplies for the Burmese people. Each family is allowed goods according to the number of family members. In front of Thet Way's house is a small market. Next door a grocery store sells dried fruit and cigars. The restaurant near their house sells Burmese noodles known as *oonoukauswe*. Peddlers sell their goods door-to-door. Today Thet Way's mother buys some doughnuts for her boys.

A peddler sells household goods.

The sweet shop.

A tea house.

20

A special treat: munching doughnuts with a friend.

An oonoukauswe restaurant.

A nearby health clinic.

Delivering newspapers. Children may deliver newspapers to add to the family income.

Thet Way's father often goes to a tea house. This is a men's place. Here men drink tea or coffee and chat and play games. Thet Way's mother meets her friends at the rationing office or market.

21

Thet Way's school is about a five-minute walk from home.

The school ground during rainy season: a playground for ducks.

Teacher and students alike shout out loud to practise correct pronunciation.

Thet Way's School

Thet Way is in the third year of primary school. His brother Thet Nay is in the first year. The school building is not large enough to hold all the students at the same time. So the first and second years go to school from 8:00 a.m. to noon. The third and fourth years go from noon to 4:00 p.m.

During the dry season, the school ground is the playground for all the children. During the rainy season, it is covered with weeds and pools. Then it becomes a playground for the ducks!

23

Thet Way's English notebook.

An earthenware water tank in the hall.

The children's board and chalk.

Thet Way's class has 57 students. They are squeezed tightly into one room. The classrooms are only partially separated by walls, so everyone has to speak up to be heard. The first class today is English. Daw Kiwensi, the teacher, leads the class. They are doing pronunciation exercises.

A Burmese language textbook.

24

English is Thet Way's favourite subject.

Thet Way works hard at English. He pays careful attention to his teacher, and he writes the new phrases in his notebook. He needs good English because he wants to become a sailor. As a poor country, Burma has strict laws limiting the movement of its citizens and their money out of the country. Usually only sailors, diplomats, and students studying abroad may leave the country.

Once abroad, a Burmese can make twenty or thirty times more money than at home. Working abroad is the only way to buy a television or car. Thet Way would like to buy a car. Then his father could drive a taxi in the city. His father wants him to study hard to become a doctor or an engineer.

Thet Way's third-year class.

Besides English, Thet Way also studies maths, Burmese, science, and social studies. In social studies, the class studies geography and history. But that is not all. The class also discusses the life and work of the people in Thet Way's neighbourhood. There are no classes for music, sports, or crafts. But sometimes the teacher sets aside time for these subjects and says, 'Let's sing some songs before we start class', or 'Why don't we play some soccer'.

Many exams await Thet Way if he wants to go to the university or to the sailors' trade school. Only one child in twenty can go on to high school, and Thet Way must pass three entrance exams between now and then. He also has to pass an exam at the end of each school year to be promoted to the next grade. His father encourages him to study hard. He says to Thet Way, 'Only the rich kids from Rangoon can pass the entrance exams for the good school'. Thet Way doesn't worry. But he studies English and maths hard because he likes them.

A top.

The boys' marbles.

Boats made of folded newspaper.

After School

Thet Way's favourite toy is a catapult. His father made it from wood and a thick rubber band. He shoots pebbles at birds. But he hasn't hit any yet.

Thet Way's pride and joy: his catapult.

Girls play apart from the boys.

The street makes a fine playground for the children. Other than an occasional water buffalo, there is little traffic.

Thet Way, Thet Nay, and their friends build a dam across a small waterway.

Thet Way and his friends also play a game like marbles with clay balls.
The goal is to hit another ball with one's own. He is good at this, but so
are his friends.

Older boys play with tops. They spin them and try to knock over other
tops. Thet Way is still not good at tops. But he is working at it so he
can play with the big boys. Girls sometimes jump over rubber strings,
or they play at home. Boys and girls almost never play together.
Sometimes they poke or tease one another — but then they run away.

Reading comics is a fun way to spend a rainy day.

Thet Way's desk is a small table.

Thet Way carries his books in a *Shan* bag.
Most Burmese carry these shoulder bags.

Playing soccer, Burma's most popular sport.

Thet Way stays home after school when it rains or when he studies. He studies on the bed, which is covered with a bamboo knitted mat.

Burma's rainy season is from June to October. During this season it rains for hours a day, so hard that you can't see anything outside the house. Thet Way and his brother entertain themselves indoors. They read comics and wrestle.

When the rain stops, the boys go outside again. They love to play soccer. They run around and kick the ball in their sandals. They are happy to be out and active.

Flowers and fruit deck a
Buddhist altar.

Thet Way's father prepares for shinbyu.

Preparing food for
the guests.

The Shinbyu Ceremony

The months of March to May are especially hot, so school closes for the
summer. This year's summer is special. Thet Way and his brother are
going to become boy monks for a time. The ceremony is called *shinbyu*.

The boys are very busy. Every day they meet with a monk. They
prepare their clothes for the ceremony. The altars are decorated with
coconut fruit, bananas, and a monk's robe. Thet Way's mother is
preparing oonoukauswe for 200 guests.

Ritual make-up made from tanaka.

Neighbours help the boys into their costumes.

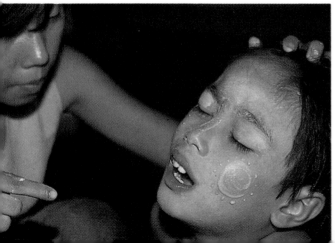

Early in the morning, neighbours gather for oonoukauswe and juice.

Thet Way and Thet Nay lead a parade to the temple.

The morning of the shinbyu festival begins with a long bath. A neighbour puts the ritual make-up on the boys' faces. They dress in costumes as beautiful as those of the kings of old Burma. Once they are dressed in their costumes, they may not walk. Their parents carry them to a beautifully decorated horse. With music playing loudly, they ride to the temple. Behind them is a parade of people carrying offerings.

Money is among the decorations.

The parade arrives at the temple.

The shinbyu ceremony. It introduces the boys to a life of self-discipline, good deeds, and inner peace.

Around the age of 19, a ceremony called *pazin* introduces them to adulthood.

Standing before the statue of Buddha in the temple.

A monk of high rank gives the boys his blessing.

The ceremony of shaving the boys' heads.

At the temple, a monk shaves the heads of the little boys. The boys are washed again. They are then dressed in red monk's robes. Now they repeat after the monk sayings in Pali. Pali is the Indian language of the ancient Buddhist texts.

Their friends and family return home. Their life in the temple begins.

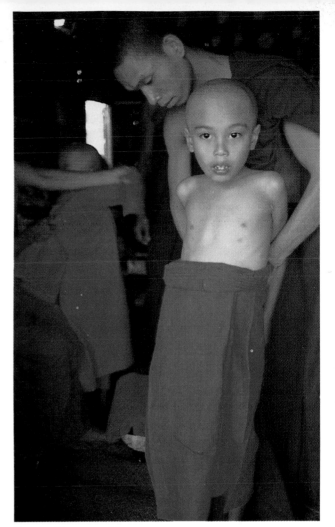

Dressed in a monk's gown, each boy is now a *coyin*, or boy monk.

The morning after the shinbyu ceremony, the temple monks are invited to the family's home. There they receive breakfast and other offerings. These offerings are signs of the family's gratitude.

A Week in the Monastery

Begging for food,
a traditional activity for monks.

The neighbours are always generous with their
breakfast offerings.

The day in the monastery begins at 5:00 a.m. The
boys awaken and wash. For an hour they recite
ancient Buddhist texts in the large hall. These texts
are called *sutras*.

No cooking is done in the temple. The boy monks
must go out and beg for their breakfast. An hour
of walking about will bring them a large bowl of
food. They must eat well now, because this is the
only meal they will have today.

In the afternoon, the monks are quite busy. They study Buddhist sutras, meditate with closed eyes, and talk quietly among themselves. After prayers, meals, and begging, the boy monks have little to do. In the afternoon, they are free to go to the garden. Actually, the boys are not supposed to play games at all. But the old monks supervising them kindly ignore their play.

The boy monks spend the afternoon with a game of cigar-butt dominoes.

The boy monks sleep on a straw mat.

A monk's life is simple and natural. The boys sleep on a mat on the floor. During the second night, Thet Nay becomes very homesick and goes home to sleep. But Thet Way is happy with his life as a grown-up. He stays the night. After a week, their parents come to take them home.

No special ceremony is needed to return to normal life. A monk says a prayer for the boys, and they change into clothes their mother has brought. They say a prayer of farewell, and their week as boy monks is over.

An old monk preaches to the boys.

Thet Nay is happy to be home. Thet Way is not so sure. He feels older and wiser after his time at the temple. He is disappointed that it is over. Eventually his cheerfulness comes back, and he chases after his younger brother. The summer of shinbyu ends.

Thet Way and Thet Nay go back to being ordinary boys. The monk makes a special prayer for this day.

The boys wear hats until their hair grows back.

The water-splashing festival is a happy time for children.

Young people splashing from their cars.

The day after the boys return home, *Thingyan* begins. Thingyan is the New Year season. This holiday includes the festival of water splashing. Some say the custom began long ago. Young girls prayed for victory for their soldiers by pouring water on them from tall trees. As time went on, Thingyan became a harvest festival.

Today young people run around town, splashing each other with buckets of water and hoses. During this three-day holiday, Thet Way and his friends splash each other silly. For three days, they don't have to worry about being scolded by their parents. They are not allowed to splash water on people who are old or ill, however.

For now, Thet Way has forgotten about his sadness after leaving the monastery. He is a boy once again.

In the temples, the Buddhist images are splashed in a very solemn ceremony. The New Year begins.

Buddhist statues are bathed in water in the temple.

Standing before Shwe Dagon Pagoda, one of Burma's largest pagodas.

A Day In Rangoon

Thet Way goes into Rangoon with his father and brother. They are visiting Shwe Dagon Pagoda. It is one of the largest pagodas in Burma. They are giving thanks for the safe birth of the boys' baby sister.

After their prayer, they go to Sule Pagoda Road. This street is in the centre of Rangoon. Thet Way asks to see buildings from the days Britain ruled Burma. There are cars and people everywhere. Thet Way and his father and brother stop for cake at a tea house. The boys want to go to a film. But the cinemas are too crowded, and they cannot get in.

The shops are filled with televisions, cassette players, cameras, electric fans, toys, and dolls — everything Thet Way wants! He is now more determined than ever to become a sailor.

A tea house in Rangoon.

A cinema. The actors speak in Burmese and English, as well as in the Chinese and Indian languages. Many are made in Hollywood.

On a street corner. There are still many buildings from the days when Burma was under British rule.

As a Buddhist country, Burma has many temples and ancient remains. One of the most important is Kyaiktiyo Pagoda. It is in the mountains near the border with Thailand.

It is a huge rock covered with gold leaf, which is a thin sheet of gold. It has a gold tower on it, and it stands at the top of a huge cliff. Even if pushed, this huge rock does not fall. According to Burmese legend, it is floating on air.

FOR YOUR INFORMATION: Burma

Official Name: Socialist Republic of the
Union of Burma

Pyidaungsu Socialist Thammada Myanma Naingngandau
(peeh-DAWNG-su socialist tah-mah-DAH mee-AN-mah NANE-nahn-doh)

Capital: Rangoon

History

A Land United and Divided

Burma is a land of many peoples living in one country. Since the Stone Age, people have migrated into Burma. Many came from central Asia down the Irrawaddy and the Salween river valleys. Burma's long rivers are separated by mountain ranges. So the same channels that first led people into Burma have also helped keep many of these people apart. Through most of its long history, both the land and the people of Burma have been divided. As a nation, Burma has had only a few short periods of unity.

The Dynasties of Burma

By 300 BC, parts of Burma were settled by the Mon people. The Mon people are related to the Khmer, who came to Cambodia. Over time, other ethnic groups migrated into what is now Burma and conquered the Mon. These groups brought outside influences to the Mon. These influences helped shape Burma into what it is today. One of these influences was the Buddhist religion. It came across the Andaman Sea from India.

In AD 1044, the first united Burmese kingdom came into being at Pagan. The Pagan king Anawratha was one of the greatest of Burma's many kings. He brought Theravada Buddhism to Pagan from the Mon. He introduced a written script into the Burmese language. He also began the Pagan Dynasty, which lasted over two hundred years.

In 1287, Kublai Khan led a Mongol invasion that destroyed the Pagan civilization. The Mongols were driven out of Burma by the Shan, a Thai-speaking people. The Shan had come to Pagan from south China. They joined with the Burmese to rule the kingdom of Ava in northern Burma. The Mon ruled their own territory in the south.

A second dynasty came into being in 1486. It was called the Toungoo Dynasty. For years Burma was jointly ruled by Mon and Shan leaders. This joint rule did not bring the many groups together, however. By 1753, all of Burma was under the rule of King Alaungpaya. His power reached far beyond the borders of his country, and he founded the Konbaung Dynasty. This would be the last dynasty to unify Burma.

Burma Under Britain

By the end of the 1700s, Burma had invaded Siam (now Thailand). Burma also turned back the Chinese and went into Assam. Assam is a neighbouring state in northeast India. This action brought Burma face to face with the British in India. Between 1824 and 1886, Burma and Britain fought three wars. During this time, Britain exiled Burma's last king and destroyed the Burmese monarchy. It also made Burma a part of British India.

The Burmese fought hard against British rule. In the late 19th and early 20th centuries, the British faced many peasant rebellions and student strikes. In 1937, Burma was separated from India and became a British crown colony, like Hong Kong. It had its own constitution. But it was still under Britain. Also, its minorities were not part of Burma as a whole.

Burma After Britain

In 1941, the Japanese invaded Burma and took control of most of the country. At first, the Japanese promised to help the Burmese fight British rule. After a while, however, the people became tired of Japan's broken promises. They organized an independence-seeking group called the Anti-Fascist People's Freedom League (AFPFL). In 1945, they helped the Allies get Japan out of Burma, and the AFPFL became the government of Burma. The AFPFL then pushed for complete independence from Britain. Finally, in 1948 the many groups and regions of British Burma became the Union of Burma.

One of the world's most remarkable sights: the hundreds of temples and pagodas that dot the 40-sq-km landscape of Pagan, one of Burma's ancient royal cities. Most were built during Pagan's 200-year 'golden' period in the 11th, 12th, and 13th centuries.

49

Burma Today

For ten years, Burma modelled its government after Britain's. It became a parliamentary democracy. The new government wanted to create a socialist nation. Communist, minority, and other groups resisted the Burmese government, however. And in 1958, splits appeared in the ruling AFPFL itself. In 1962, the military set up a new government. In 1973, that government held a national vote. This vote made the government an elected one. The elections also gave Burma a new constitution and a new name — the Socialist Republic of the Union of Burma.

The dream of a unified *modern* Burma may be more real than ever. But Burma has a history of being divided. It has been divided by its own geography, by its own different peoples, and by the foreign powers that have used Burma for their own purposes. Under its form of socialism, called the Burmese Way of Socialism, Burma is trying to unite its many peoples.

Population and Ethnic Groups

The Burmese Nationals

Burma has a population of about 35 million. The Burmese government estimates that it will reach 50 million by the year 2000.

Burma is a land of many nationalities and peoples. There are as many as 50 national groups. Among these groups, over one hundred languages and dialects are spoken. The largest group is the Burmese. There are over 25 million Burmese nationals in Burma. They make up about 68% of the population. They live throughout the country, but they live mainly in the lower, less mountainous regions.

The Seven States

Throughout its history, Burma has been made up of several major peoples other than Burmese. Seven of these peoples have states within Burma. Each state is named after one of these groups. Each state reflects the character of the group after which it is named. Still, these groups also live side by side throughout Burma as a whole. Here are the seven peoples.

The Shans
There are over three million Shans. They are Burma's second largest people. They are ethnically related to the Thai people of Thailand. They live mainly in the Shan Plateau region, which borders Thailand.

The Karens
There are about 2.5 million Karens. Many of them have become assimilated with the Burmese and Mons.

The Rakhines
There are about 1.5 million Rakhines in Burma. Like the Burmese nationals, the Rakhines use Burmese as their national language. But they speak in a

different tone and accent. Their state is in the coastal region of the Rakhine, or Arakan, Mountains.

The Kachins
There are about one million Kachins in Burma. Many of them live in Kachin state and the northern part of Shan state.

The Mons
The Mons also number about one million. They are one of Burma's oldest civilizations. They live throughout southeast Burma.

The Chins
There are also about one million Chins in Burma. They live mainly in the Chin Hills and in the dry zone west of the River Irrawaddy.

The Kayahs
The Kayahs are one of the smallest national groups with a state of their own. They number about 150,000.

Other Minorities

Burma also has large ethnic Chinese and Indian populations. There are around one million Chinese (3% of the population) and about three-quarters of a million Indians (2%) in Burma. Chinese and Indian influences in Burma have been felt in business and religion. There is also a minority with its origins in Bangladesh.

Religion

About 85% of the people of Burma are Buddhist. Minority religions include Islam, Christianity, and traditional native religious practices. In the Rakhine, or Arakan, area near Bangladesh there are many Muslims. The first Christians to visit Burma came over 300 years ago, but they did not convert many Burmese to Christianity. There is a Church of Burma in Rangoon, however. It has about 30,000 members and a large cathedral. Many Chin, Karen, and Kachin peoples are Christian.

Buddhism is the religion of Burma. This shows in the architecture and way of life of most Burmese, who are Theravada Buddhists. They see Buddha as a teacher, not a god. And Buddhism is a way of teaching and learning. Buddhist teaching helps people to find the best way to live.

Throughout history, kings and monks in Burma supported and honoured each other. Today the government of Burma does not call attention to Buddhism but does not interfere with its practice. Some Buddhists believe that one day a leader will come to prepare the world for the next Buddha. They believe this leader will create a paradise on earth and the Buddha will preach to the people there. Scriptures say this event is still 2,500 years away. But some interpret them to say it is at hand.

Buddhists in Burma believe that all living things are reborn. Throughout their lives, Buddhists earn merits or demerits according to how well they live. Their next life will reflect the merits they earned in this life. The greatest human accomplishment is to return as a monk. The final goal, though, is to reach nirvana. At this stage the person does not return at all. Merit is earned by living a life detached from worldly concerns. As people grow older, they begin to detach themselves from this world in preparation for leaving it.

After performing an act of merit, a person will ring a bell to spread its benefit to all who can hear it. There is even more merit in sharing a good work. Becoming a boy monk is a generous act of merit for a young boy. Usually he will share the merit he earns with his mother.

Because Burmese believe that their lot in life is payment for deeds in the life before, they accept the difficulties that it brings. Even the poorest Burmese give honour to Buddha by building and lavishly decorating pagodas in his honour.

The Burmese Way of Life

The values taught by Buddhist monks affect greatly the way Burmese people approach their lives. For example, they feel that to hurry shows a lack of trust in fate. So they are patient. They also expect others to be patient. Their long history of isolation has kept them from seeing the hurry of the Western world. Even now, when they are exposed to it, they do not feel it is a better way to live. Giving to honour Buddha is not seen as sacrifice; it is seen as a joyful release from greed. The Burmese enjoy their giving. In the past, they have devoted much of their country's wealth to honouring Buddha. Though many of the people lacked food and shelter, millions of pounds were spent on building and decorating pagodas. Even those people who lived without basic needs lovingly honoured their teacher. Buddhist values teach them that they should detach themselves from earthly concerns. So going without and honouring Buddha are not cause for bad feelings. Even today about 20% of Burma's wealth is spent on rebuilding and gilding pagodas and statues. Colonial powers have at times tried to convince people that serving the state was a good way to honour Buddha. But the Burmese have been sure in their belief that such was not the case.

Government

Burma became a one-party socialist republic in 1962. In 1973, the Burmese people voted for a new constitution. Under this constitution, Burma's official name was changed. The Union of Burma became the Socialist Republic of the Union of Burma. The constitution also set up national elections.

Burma has a People's Assembly of 475 members. All members are elected nationally every four years. The People's Assembly in turn elects members of smaller ruling groups. From these groups the prime minister, president, and other leaders are selected. Local elections are also held throughout the country.

Burma is divided into seven states and seven divisions. These 14 regions have their own governing bodies. And yet they are controlled centrally by the Burmese government — much like the separate states, provinces, and territories of the US or Canada. The *state* names reflect some of Burma's minority peoples. And the *divisions* are meant to reflect the character of the majority ethnic Burmese people. However, the many races and peoples that make up Burma today are scattered throughout the country as a whole.

The Burma Socialist Programme Party (BSPP) is the country's only legal political party. Nonmembers may run for public office. But all candidates must be approved by the BSPP. Burma's history is filled with conflicts among its many ethnic groups and with foreign countries. Setting up a socialist government has unified the many peoples and groups of Burma into one national body. This has been a difficult goal to achieve. Many of Burma's ethnic groups want independence from the central government. Some of these groups have political organizations. Many of them have used force to make their feelings known to the government.

Burma lived and suffered under the rule of others for many years. This changed in 1948, when Burma became independent. Since then, every Burmese government has tried to get rid of foreign economic and political power. This has meant nationalizing, or taking over, foreign-owned businesses. It has also meant being strictly neutral in world affairs. At times, this attitude toward other countries has cut off Burma from the rest of the world. Today, Burma has good relations with many countries, including the US, Canada, the People's Republic of China, West Germany, Japan, and many other countries in Europe and Asia. Many travel restrictions still apply for Burmese and foreigners alike. For example, foreign tourists may stay in Burma no longer than seven days. Business people may stay longer, but they must apply to the government in advance.

Most restrictions are for areas where rebel fighting is going on. The government's hold on these areas may not be very strong. One such area is the 'Golden Triangle', where Laos, Thailand, and Burma meet. There, rebel activity is strong, and there is much drug trafficking. Another trouble spot for the Burmese government is on the Rakhine, or Arakan, coast of the Bay of Bengal. This area is near Bangladesh. In 1978, thousands of Muslim Burmese fled from here to Bangladesh, which is a Muslim nation. Later, most returned to Burma. Despite the trouble spots and restrictions, tourists enjoy Burma greatly.

Education

After one year of kindergarten, there are four years of primary school, four years of junior high school, and two years of senior high school. Only four years of school are required. In the past, Burma has had few schools and teachers. Because of this, only 66% of Burmese adults can read. The government has been building more schools, however. It is also encouraging attendance at the lower grades.

About 84% of all primary age children (ages 6-9) are now attending school, mostly in half-day sessions. The literacy rate is therefore expected to rise in the years to come. In rural areas, Buddhist temple schools also teach young children basic skills.

Students must pass exams to move from one year to the next and to get into junior and senior high school. Places in the upper grades are limited. A child entering primary school has only a 1-in-20 chance of getting into high school. After high school there are three choices for further education: vocational or teacher training schools (each 1-3 years), or university education (4-7 years). Competition is very stiff for these schools.

In addition to Burmese and English, students study the history and culture of their area and people. They also study maths, science, social studies, geography, and history.

Language

Burma is a country of many languages. There are over 100 languages and dialects spoken by the many peoples of Burma. They are quite different from each other, and yet they exist side by side. The national language is Burmese, which is related to the Tibetan language. It is spoken by about 80% of the population. Many people use their own language at home and Burmese outside. The schools teach both Burmese and English, which is Burma's official second language. In fact, enough people speak English to support two daily English newspapers in Rangoon.

Sports and Recreation

Burmese enjoy watching and taking part in sports. By far, soccer is the favourite spectator sport in Burma. Boxing is also quite popular. But it is not the boxing that most Westerners know. Like boxing elsewhere in Southeast Asia, Burmese boxing means much more than punching your opponent. Boxers may kick with their feet and jab with their knees. Boxing matches take place at many events, such as *pwes*, which are Burmese festivals. Burmese are thought to be a very calm people. But they can be as excited about boxing as people in other countries are about soccer. At one pwe in Rangoon, supporters of the defeated boxer became so enraged that they wrecked an entire arena. The rest of the night's matches had to be cancelled.

One extremely popular Burmese sport is *chinlone*. This sport is played everywhere in Burma by people of all ages. It is played with a ball made of woven cane. Up to six players stand in a circle. The aim of the game is to keep the ball from hitting the ground. The players may use any part of their bodies other than their hands and arms to keep the ball in the air. They kick the ball into the air with their feet, knees, elbows, and shoulders. When the ball falls behind the back, even calves and heels get into the act!

There is little TV in Burma, but Burmese love the cinema. Films are shown in the major languages of Burma: Burmese, English, Chinese, and Indian. Burma produces many films of its own. Most films from the West are quite old. Hollywood films are favourites. In addition to films, Burmese enjoy pwes, or street theatre festivals. You can read more about pwes in the 'Arts and Crafts' discussion below.

Arts and Crafts

For a long time, Burma was isolated from the Western world and its markets. That is one reason why most people here are not familiar with the beautiful handwork of Burma's people. Burmese craftspeople are skilled in leather, silver, and clay. Burmese lacquerware goes back to the 11th century. Traditional Burmese lacquerware is carved with scenes from the stories of Buddha. Many types of lacquerware articles are available. They include boxes, vases, trays, bowls, and even coffee tables.

The elephant is highly valued in Burma. Even today, it hauls logs from the forests. It is illegal to hunt elephants. But ivory from tusks is available from elephants that die naturally. Burmese artists carve traditional designs onto whole tusks. They also make figurines, powder boxes, and lamp bases.

Burmese skills in carving also show up in beautiful wood carvings. These carvings decorate the roofs, walls, doors, and windows of pagodas and monasteries. Carvers also make statues of monks, figurines, screens, and furniture.

Every pagoda in Burma has bells. They are struck to tell the world of good deeds done. There are triangular bells, which twirl when struck and ring with a sweet rising and falling tone. And there are gongs. Some are slung from carved ivory or wood elephant trunks. They are prized as dinner gongs.

Burmese weavers make a lovely cloth called *Cheik*. Although this is an old art, Burmese weavers now use some techniques from Japan, the West, and Thailand. These fabrics are silk with raised wavy or twisted patterns.

Drama, dance, and music are a major part of Burmese life. One cultural form, the pwe, combines drama with dance and music. A pwe is a form of theatre performed at festivals. A pwe can occur at formal events, such as weddings, religious festivals, or a monk's funeral. Or it can take place at less formal events, such as street fairs or sporting events. There are many different kinds of pwe, but any pwe can easily last all night. A *zat pwe* is a dance drama. It presents tales filled with characters from ancient Hindu and Buddhist tales. But the concerns are modern. Other kinds of pwe use comedy, singing, and puppets. Burmese consider a skilled puppeteer to be as much an artist as a zat pwe performer.

Burmese music is a part of any pwe. The instruments include a woodwind instrument like an oboe, a bamboo flute, brass cymbals, bamboo clappers, drums and gongs, both tuned to play melodies, and a Burmese harp, which is the only instrument played by a woman.

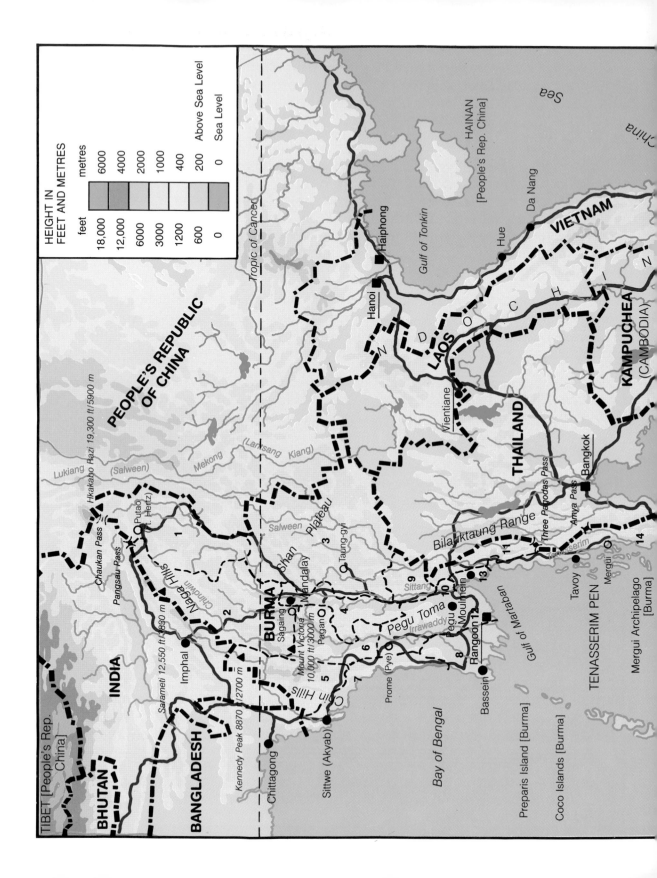

HEIGHT IN
FEET AND METRES

feet	metres		
18,000	6000		Above Sea Level
12,000	4000		
6000	2000		
3000	1000		
1200	400		
600	200		
0	0		Sea Level

Tropic of Cancer

TIBET [People's Rep. China]

BHUTAN

BANGLADESH

INDIA

PEOPLE'S REPUBLIC OF CHINA

Hkakabo Razi 19,300 ft/5900 m

Lukiang *(Salween)*

Mekong

(Lantsang Kiang)

Chaukan Pass

Pangsau Pass

Putao
(Mt. Hertz)

Saramati 12,550 ft/3830 m

Imphal

Kennedy Peak 8870 ft/2700 m

Chittagong

Sittwe (Akyab)

Naga Hills

Chindwin

Chin Hills

1

2

Sagaing

Mount Victoria
10,000 ft/3000 m

Mandalay

Pagan

5

6

7

Prome (Pye)

8

Bassein

BURMA

Shan

Salween

Plateau

Taung-gyi

3

4

Pegu Toma

Irrawaddy

Sittang

9

10

11

13

12

Pegu

Rangoon

Moulmein

Bilauktaung Range

Three Pagodas Pass

Amya Pass

14

Tavoy

Mergui

Tenasserim

Mergui Archipelago [Burma]

TENASSERIM PEN

Gulf of Martaban

Bay of Bengal

Preparis Island [Burma]

Coco Islands [Burma]

LAOS

Hanoi

Haiphong

Gulf of Tonkin

HAINAN
[People's Rep. China]

Hue

Da Nang

VIETNAM

INDOCHINA

Vientiane

THAILAND

Bangkok

KAMPUCHEA
(CAMBODIA)

China

Sea

BURMA – Political and Physical

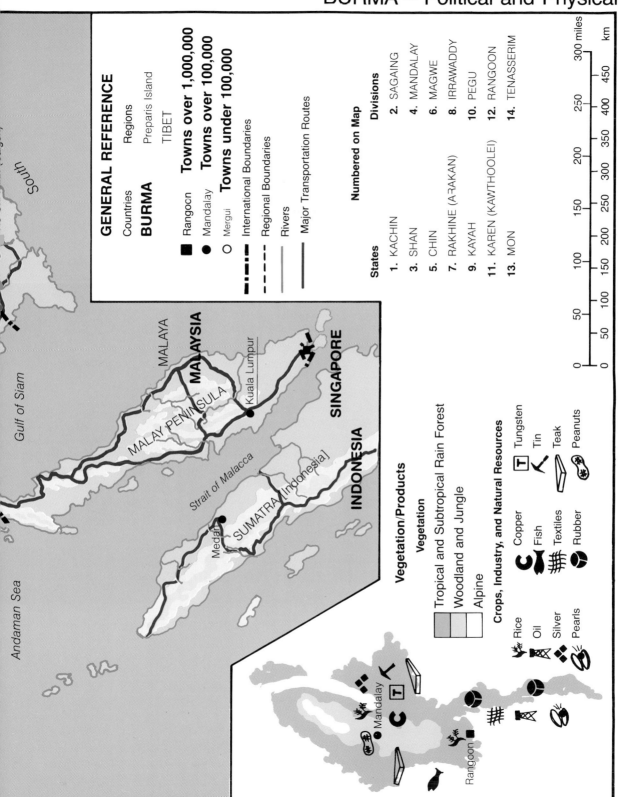

GENERAL REFERENCE

Countries   **Regions**

BURMA   Preparis Island

■ Rangoon — Towns over 1,000,000

● Mandalay — Towns over 100,000

○ Mergui — Towns under 100,000

TIBET

▪▪▪ International Boundaries

--- Regional Boundaries

— Rivers

— Major Transportation Routes

Numbered on Map

States

1. KACHIN
3. SHAN
5. CHIN
7. RAKHINE (ARAKAN)
9. KAYAH
11. KAREN (KAWTHOOLEI)
13. MON

Divisions

2. SAGAING
4. MANDALAY
6. MAGWE
8. IRRAWADDY
10. PEGU
12. RANGOON
14. TENASSERIM

Vegetation/Products

Vegetation

Tropical and Subtropical Rain Forest

Woodland and Jungle

Alpine

Crops, Industry, and Natural Resources

Rice

Oil

Silver

Pearls

C Copper

Fish

Textiles

Rubber

T Tungsten

Tin

Teak

Peanuts

Gulf of Siam

Andaman Sea

South

MALAYA

MALAYSIA

MALAY PENINSULA

Kuala Lumpur

SINGAPORE

Strait of Malacca

SUMATRA [Indonesia]

Medan

INDONESIA

Mandalay

Rangoon

km

0   50   100   150   200   250   300 miles

0   50   100   150   200   250   300   350   400   450   km

Land

Burma is the largest country on the mainland of Southeast Asia. Its area is about 678,500 sq km. It is nearly three times larger than the UK. It stretches 2,090 km from north to south and 925 km from east to west at its widest points. On land, it is bordered by Bangladesh and India to the west, China to the northeast, and Laos and Thailand to the east. It faces the Bay of Bengal and the Andaman Sea on the west and south. The bulk of its area is on the Asian mainland. Its southernmost tip snakes its way down a stretch of the Malay Peninsula. This stretch is the Tenasserim Peninsula. Burma shares this narrow strip of land with southern Thailand.

Burma is a land of alternating mountain ranges and river valleys. The three main mountain ranges are the Rakhine or Arakan Yoma, the Pegu Yoma, and the Shan Plateau. The three main rivers are the Irrawaddy, the Sittang, and the Salween. In its ancient past, the rivers conducted migrants from Asia down into what is today Burma. The mountains formed natural barriers between these groups.

Burma is at the eastern edge of the Himalaya Mountains. Therefore, some of its mountains are among the highest in the world. For example, the peak of Hkakabo Razi, near the border between Burma and the Tibet region of China, is over 5,900 m high. This makes it the highest peak in Southeast Asia. Even today, the mountains and rivers form natural barriers both within Burma and between Burma and its neighbours.

Climate

Burma has a tropical monsoon climate. Along the coasts and river deltas, including Rangoon, average temperatures range from 21°C during the cool season to 32°C. During the hot season, March-May, temperatures may go as high as 43°C. The monsoon season is between May and September. The average annual rainfall along the coast is about 500 cm. The central river valley and the Shan Plateau are much more dry. There, the average annual rainfall is about 77 cm.

Industry, Agriculture, and Natural Resources

Burma is mainly an agricultural country. About 76% of Burma's people live in rural areas, and about 65% of the labour force works in agriculture. Rice is its main crop. Before World War II, Burma was the world's largest exporter of rice (3.3 million tonnes per year). In recent years, rice exports have averaged only about 800,000 tonnes per year. Burma offers the world as many as 60 grades or types of rice and rice products.

About 15% of Burma's total land is made up of forests reserved for conservation and for state timber operations. Another 35% of Burma's land is also wooded, for a total of 50% forest land. Most of the forest land is in the mountains. There, the rainfall is heaviest. Forest products rank second to rice as Burma's source of foreign trade. Before World War II, Burma produced about 76% of the world's total supply of teak. Today, that figure has actually grown, to 90%. Burma also manufactures many objects out of teakwood.

In addition to timber, Burma's natural resources include oil, tin, tungsten, copper, silver, and precious stones. Of Burma's many precious stones, sapphires and rubies are the most famous. In fact, rubies of the finest red colour are known worldwide as 'Burma Rubies', regardless of where the rubies are from. Burma is also known for nephrite and jadeite. These are the two minerals from which jade figures are made. In 1982, the world's largest piece of jade was discovered in Burma. It weighed 33 tonnes!

For years after independence, Burma cut itself off from trade with other countries. Today, however, Burma has trade relations with many countries, including Canada, the US, Western Europe, the USSR, and other countries of Eastern Europe and Asia. Burma's major trading partners are Japan, Singapore, China, and West Germany.

Rangoon

Rangoon is quite new as a capital city. Though it has a long history as a fishing village, it has been Burma's capital only since 1875. Most building there took place in the late 19th century. It was heavily damaged in World War II. Today it is completely rebuilt. It is a modern city with large office buildings, cinemas, taxis, and buses. But mostly it is a city of lakes, valleys, and tree-lined streets. It has both Chinese and Indian sections of town as well as Burmese. The Rangoon Zoo, with its snake charmer shows and elephant rides, is a favourite spot for visitors and children. The River Rangoon, where rice is loaded and stored, runs through the city.

A vast array of statues, temples, carvings, shrines, and smaller pagodas surround the Shwe Dagon Pagoda in Rangoon.

The Shwe Dagon Pagoda sits high on a hill. According to legend, the first pagoda was built on this site over 2,000 years ago. Buddhists from all over the world visit the Shwe Dagon Pagoda because four hairs from Buddha are enshrined in it. Its spire, which rises 100 m above its platform, is visible throughout Rangoon. The base is 430 m around. The top of the spire is covered with 8,688 sheets of gold. Each sheet is 0.3 sq m and is worth about £6,000. The gold is encrusted with 500 diamonds and 200 other jewels. The stairways leading to the Shwe Dagon Pagoda house hundreds of small shops selling souvenirs and food.

Currency

The chief unit of Burmese currency is the *kyat* (pronounced 'chat'). One chat equals 100 *pyas*.

Like travel, the flow of currency out of Burma is strictly controlled by the government. Any amount of foreign currency may be brought *into* Burma, so long as it is recorded with the government. However, only that amount or less may be brought out. Also, the import and export of Burmese currency is forbidden.

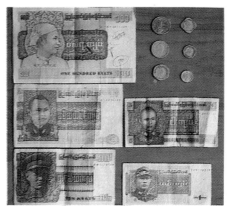

Burmese currency.

Burmese Emigrants

Burmese come to the United Kingdom for a variety of reasons. Some come as students. Most Burmese cannot afford a private education, however. And because the flow of money out of Burma is restricted, their government cannot offer financial aid. There are therefore few Burmese students in the United Kingdom — as few as 200. They come here mainly to learn English and study medicine. Of the 500 or 600 Burmese passport holders in this country, most are doctors in London, Scotland, Wales and Ireland. It is thought there are fewer than 50 businessmen from Burma here at any one time. Not many Burmese tourists visit the UK and those who do usually come to see relatives working here. Emigration to this country is very difficult because of our strict immigration laws.

Glossary of Useful Burmese Terms

The Burmese language has an alphabet and script of its own. They are quite different from the Roman alphabet that we use in modern English. Many of the words are spelled in a way that makes them easier to pronounce. These spellings are not meant to look like the actual Burmese words.

chay-zoo pyu-baa .... please
chay-zoo tin-baa deh .... thank you
coyin (COY-in) .... a novice, or boy, monk
Daw .... 'aunt'; a respectful way of addressing any adult woman, married or single
hey .... hello
kah-oong deh .... good
kwin pyu baa .... excuse me
kyat (chat) .... the main unit of Burmese currency
longyi (long-gee) .... sarong; long cloth skirt worn by men and women

maa yeh laa?	how are you?
min ga la baa	good morning/afternoon/evening
nirvana (ner-VAH-nah)	in Buddhism, the highest spiritual state or goal
oonoukauswe (ooh-now-kah-sweh)	Burmese noodles
pwe (pway)	Burmese celebration or theatre
shinbyu (shin-byoo)	a Buddhist ceremony for novice monks
ta min	rice
tanaka (thah-nah-kah)	Burmese make-up used on the arms and face; plant ground into white powder for make-up
thu	he/she
thwah pah taw may	good-bye
U (oo)	'uncle'; a respectful way of addressing any adult male
zat pwe	dance drama based on ancient Hindu and Buddhist tales

More Books About Burma

Here are some more books about Burma. If you are interested in them, check your library. They may be helpful in doing research for the following 'Things to Do'.

Burma by G. Houghton and J. Wakefield (Macmillan, 1988)
Collins Illustrated Guide to Burma (Collins, 1988)
Let's Visit Burma by Aung San Suu Kyi (Macmillan, 1985)

Things to Do - Research Projects

Since it gained freedom in 1948, Burma has cut itself off from the rest of the world. After years of oppression by outsiders, its goal was to rid itself of foreign influence. And during these years Burma has been known as a country that is rich in human and natural resources but poor in its economic development. Today, Burma wants to expand its trade relations with other countries. As you read about Burma, keep in mind the importance of current facts. Some of the research projects that follow need accurate, up-to-date information. Two publications your library may have will tell you about recent magazine and newspaper articles on many topics:

The Times Index
Keesing's Record of World Events

For accurate answers to questions about such topics of current interest as Burma's relationship with the outside world, look up *Burma* in these two publications. They will lead you to the most up-to-date information you can find.

1. Use your library resources to learn about Buddhism. What values does it promote that you also hold?

2. How is the New Year in Burma celebrated? How does it compare with your New Year's celebration?

3. Write a short report about a resource or industry important to the Burmese economy. Be sure your information is current, at least within the year.

4. Many national groups make up Burma today. Some of them are discussed in this book. Others, including the Wa and the Padaung, may be less well known. Choose one group. Use library resources to find out more about that group, its culture and beliefs, how it fits in with Burmese life as a whole, and in what other countries, if any, it also lives. Report your findings to your classmates in a short paper or oral presentation.

More Things to Do — Activities

These projects are designed to encourage you to think more about Burma. They offer ideas for interesting group or individual projects you can do at school or home.

1. If you were going to talk to Thet Way or any other child from Burma, what questions would you ask?

2. Why do you think it's important to study the religion of Burma to understand its people?

3. Thet Way's father says that the chance for education in the trades or professions is restricted mostly to the children of rich people. How does this situation compare with opportunities in your country?

4. How does your life compare with Thet Way's? Write a paragraph describing the ways in which you are the same or different.

5. The government of Burma restricts the rights of its people to leave the country. Other countries do this, too. What benefit do you think this has for the people? What harm does it do?

6. If you would like a pen friend in Burma, write to these people:

International Friendship League
Pen-Friend Service
Saltash
Cornwall

Friends by Post
6 Bollin Court,
Macclesfield Road
Wilmslow
Cheshire

Be sure to tell them what country you want your pen friend to be from. Also include your full name and address.

'Thwah pah taw may!'

Index

FRANKLIN PIERCE COLLEGE LIBRARY

00104203

DATE DUE

MAR 2 2 '99			
MAY 11	2001	ILL 7527204	IBS
GAYLORD			PRINTED IN U.S.A.